Car C

Learn How to Take Care of Your Car to Keep It in Tip-Top Condition for as Long as Possible While also Reducing the Bills Considerably

By Zack Keever

Contents

Thank you for buying this book and I hope that you will find it useful. If you will want to share your thoughts on this book, you can do so by leaving a review on the Amazon page, it helps me out a lot.

Chapter 1: Tips and Suggestions for a Dependable Car

A car is a costly financial investment, so understanding how to maintain your car in great shape could spare you heaps of cash. In general, the expense of owning a car is a lot greater than numerous people may believe-- there is the expense of car insurance coverage, taxes, car loan interest, repair work, fuel expenses, and the expense of the car itself. By adopting all or just a few of these car care ideas, you could start sparing a substantial quantity of time and cash.

Simply a bit of time devoted to research could spare you future repair work and heaps of cash. You do not have to be mechanically savvy to spot typical car issues. You simply have to be able to utilize your senses of sight and smell.

Have a look Around

Are there discolorations beneath your car? Drips? They might not be an issue; however, if you see damp areas, it could be a sign of something even more severe. Which color is the fluid you are seeing? Is it orange, blue yellowish green? Then it might point to a radiator leakage, overheated engine damage, or a water pump which requires repair work. Leakages like these ought to be dealt with rapidly.

Black oily fluid or dark brown might point to oil leakage. A bad seal or gasket could induce this kind of leakage. These kinds of repair work can cost a lot, so it's an excellent idea to take your car to a mechanic you believe.

A red oily area might point to transmission leakage or power steering fluid leakage. In some cases, you are going to see clear fluid, which is typically only condensation and absolutely nothing to stress over. If you see light smoke originating from your wheel as you are driving, it might imply that you have a brake which is stuck, and you ought to pull over.

Any kind of smoke suggests that you have to see a mechanic.

Use Your Nose

Do not hesitate to smell around and see if you could identify an issue with your car. In case you smell burned toast, it might be an electrical shortage or burning insulation. Do not risk driving it. In case you smell a rotten egg odor, it's very likely the catalytic converter, and it is going to have to be fixed.

A thick sharp smell is frequently a sign of burning oil. Take a look beneath the car to see if you can identify a leakage. You might additionally see a bluish smoke originating from your car's tailpipe-- you want to have this examined ASAP.

In case you smell gas after your car falls short to kick off, the engine might have ended up being flooded. Wait a couple of minutes and attempt once again. In case you continue to discover a gas smell, you might have a leakage someplace in your fuel system, which could be harmful, so have your car taken to a mechanic immediately.

These easy pointers are going to assist in informing you of a possible issue with your car that ought to be resolved.

Chapter 2: How to Correctly Inspect Your Fluids

Part of keeping your car in tip-top shape is to ensure you routinely inspect your levels of fluids. As a matter of fact, tracking of these levels is crucial to your car health. It's an excellent idea to read your owner's handbook. There ought to be diagrams of the engine there which are going to show you where to inspect all the essential fluids. It's a fantastic means to get an idea of where vital fluids could be discovered. You can additionally utilize the web to bring up photos that can assist you.

Engine Oil

1. You'll locate towards the front of the engine a cap marked "Oil." Examine your oil with the engine off. Get rid of the dipstick

2. Rub the oil off with a rag

3. Place the dipstick back in

4. Draw it out and get your reading

5. There are going to be 2 marks on the dipstick-- maximum and minimum -- anything in-between indicates that your oil is fine. Beneath the minimum, and you want to include oil. In older cars, it's an excellent idea to examine your oil each number of weeks. In more recent cars, inspect once a month.

Transmission Oil

In case you have an automatic transmission, you are going to need to find a dipstick to examine your fluid level. It's normally discovered towards the rear of the engine. There are various approaches for inspecting transmission fluids, which could be discovered in the owner's handbook. For the majority of cars, they need to be running, and the transmission has to be in park or neutral. To get a real reading, the transmission ought to be heated up, so take it for a brief drive to bring it up to running temperature level. Make sure to check this once a year.

Engine Coolant

You must never ever open the radiator cap when the engine is hot. You could be splashed by the hot coolant and suffer major burns. Most cars have an overflow bottler with noticeable level markings. You ought to make certain your coolant is in between these markings.

Power Steering Fluid

Your car utilizes oil to help with the power steering. This liquid ought to be inspected frequently. Typically it is examined at the pump; however, in some cases, the reservoir is separate and far from the pump.

Brake Fluid

The majority of the more recent cars permit you to examine the brake fluid levels without ever needing to touch the master cylinder cap. There are markings on the side of the reservoir, identifying numerous levels. As you are removing the cover, make sure that nothing gets on the paint.

Windshield Washer Fluid

You are going to see the container which contains the blue fluid that's wonderful for maintaining your windshield tidy. The majority of the reservoirs are noticeably marked. Nevertheless, in a few of the more recent cars, the reservoir is buried, rendering it difficult to see. Simply pull the top off and begin filling. A funnel could render it a lot simpler to fill your washer liquid and other liquids.

Chapter 3: Important Summertime Car Maintenance Tips

Prior to jumping into the car and going out on that summertime trip, it's an excellent idea to make certain your car is in a ready-to-go condition. Besides, there's absolutely nothing worse than resting on the side of the roadway awaiting a tow truck when what you intended to do was spending a day on the beach.

1. Examine Your Fluids - Run your car for a couple of minutes, and after that, inspect the oil. It ought to be in the okay range and it ought to additionally be tidy on your dipstick. Oil switches are suggested at various intervals varying from 3,000 miles to 7,500 miles. Examine your owner's handbook for the suggestions for your car. In case the dipstick is at the add mark, you want to include oil. Despite the mileage, if your oil is unclean, you want to think about an oil change.

2. Examine Your Windshield Wiper Blades - Excellent wiper blades are going to be a genuine advantage throughout summertime thunderstorms and rainstorms, which could take place without much warning. Winter season conditions have a tendency to make blades tough and ineffective. Examine all your fluid levels, as well as wiper fluid to make certain all the things are topped up prior to leaving.

3. Know Your Tires-- You ought to be aware of the correct tire inflation. You could discover this in your car documents, tire documents, or on the tire sidewall. Then get your tire pressure gauge and inspect their inflation. The warmth of summertime is going to boost your tire pressure, so it's a great idea to test prior to driving far.

In case you are driving with underinflated tires, you are risking a blowout, while a tire which is overinflated places you in danger of hydroplaning in rainy weather conditions. Appropriately inflated tires are going to boost the efficiency of your fuel by as much as 3%, so there's a genuine advantage to making certain you examine your tires.

While at it, take a moment to inspect the tire tread. Utilize a cent and stick it in the gaps with the head face down. If you are able to see the head, it's time for brand-new tires.

4. Go to Your Mechanic-- A mechanic visit is a great idea prior to any long journey. Your car is going to require routine tune-ups and routine filter and oil changes.

5. Examine Hoses and Belts -- Look for heavy wear or splitting and replace what needs replacing.

6. Be Prepared-- Constantly bring an emergency set with you that consists of a first aid kit, blankets, air compressors, jumper cables, and it is additionally a great idea to bring energy and water bars.

Chapter 4: Winter Season Car-Maintenance Tips

Winter season brings along an entire brand-new list of worries for your car. The intensity of the winter season depends upon where you live. While more recent cars need less intervention from us people, they still have to have to be ready for the winter season. By executing all or a few of these car care pointers, you could start to conserve a considerable quantity of cash.

1. Watch the Tire Pressure-- Tire pressure, is going to go down when the temperature level drops. When you maintain your tires appropriately inflated, you are going to get better fuel economy, and it is going to assist against blowouts additionally.

2. Maintain Your Fuel Tank Above One-Quarter-- On older cars, this was done to guarantee that the fuel lines did not freeze. While it does not take place as frequently with brand-new cars, it could still occur, so why not guarantee that it does not. additionally, throughout winter season driving, it's

an excellent idea to be ready if you end up being stranded.

3. Inspect Your Fluids-- Some of your car's liquids are impacted by winter season conditions. Take a couple of minutes to examine your car's cooling system, and each year, you ought to do a coolant flush. Cooling system failure is the primary reason for the engine-related breakdown, that could result in costly repairs. You'll want to include antifreeze at a 50/50 ratio of water/antifreeze. You ought to purchase an antifreeze ball tester so that you could inspect your ratios during the winter and include antifreeze whenever needed. Make certain your windscreen washer liquid is topped up with winter season liquid.

4. Examine Your Battery-- Older batteries could have a problem throughout the winter season with the cold. Make certain your terminal posts do not have any rust since when the posts are rusted, it could render it tougher for the battery to get the car going. When there's exceptionally cold weather, the life span of the battery could be reduced. Lastly, ensure you constantly have jumper cables, simply if your battery dies.

5. Do an Oil Change-- Even if your car isn't quite due for an oil change, now's a great time to do an oil change. With older cars, lighter weight oil could be utilized to keep your car's parts much better lubed throughout the winter season. More recent cars utilize lighter weight oil year-round.

6. Change your Windscreen Wiper Blades-- Altering your wiper blades at the beginning of the winter is going to guarantee they are brand-new. Winter season wiper blades do a much greater job of pressing the slush off your windscreen and scraping the ice away.

7. Put Snow Tires On-- Winter season driving conditions imply that you have to have great traction. Based upon what you drive and where you live, snow tires are typically an excellent financial investment. In certain locations where snowfall is limited, you could get away with a strong all-season radial tire.

8. Bring an Emergency Set-- Your emergency set ought to consist of cold-weather equipment like jumper cables, flares, hats and gloves, flashlight, and standard tools.

Chapter 5: Tips to Prolong Your Car's Life

Maintaining your car in the first-class condition indicates you can decrease the expenses of repair work, and you could unwind since you understand you could depend upon your car.

1. Your Car Break-In Duration

You invested your hard-earned cash in purchasing your dream car, so you wish to look after it in a way that is going to offer you as many years of trusted transport as possible. Here are certain things to remember as soon as you are the happy brand-new owner of that car.

- Throughout the initial 1000 miles, you ought to maintain your speed beneath 55mph or 88kpm or whatever the producer suggests.

- Never ever allow your brand-new car be idle for extended periods both throughout the break-in and during its life. Idling does not send out ample oil across the engine.

- Throughout the break-in, stay clear of heavy loads, like trailer towing, throughout the break-in duration.

- When speeding up, maintain the engine beneath 3000 rpm for the initial couple of hours of your driving.

2. Drive With Care Every Day

You ought to drive your car with care daily, not only throughout the break-in durations.

- Throughout start-up, do not race your car engine, particularly in the cold, as it includes years of deterioration to the engine.

- You must not allow your car idle to warm up the engine. Since the engine isn't running at peak temperature levels, the fuel combustion is insufficient, inducing an accumulation of soot on the cylinder walls, polluting oil, and damaging other elements.

- Moving to neutral at red lights minimizes the stress on the engine.

- When it is exceptionally cold or hot, stay clear of driving at high speeds or speeding up too rapidly. This behavior results in the requirement for repair work more regularly.

- You could prolong your tire's life by driving cautiously. Expect posted speed limitations and comply. Stay clear of quick starts, stops, and turns. Do not burn rubber, stay clear of striking curbs, and stay clear of potholes.

3. When You are Stuck, Relax

When one becomes stuck, the initial reaction is to rock the car by going reverse, and then forward, while also spinning the tires. These acts are all right for a really brief time period, however, if you are actually stuck, call a tow truck due to the fact that the damage you could do is going to far surpass what the expense of tow truck is going to be.

4. Go Light With Your Keys

Does your keychain appear as it may be utilized as an anchor? All those keys dangling off the ignition place unneeded stress on the ignition, and that could result in the ignition tumbler wear. It's ideal if you can have your ignition key separate, or at the minimum, make certain that you have the weight on your keychain down.

5. Put in the time to discover the very best car insurance provider

Regardless of how mindful you are, catastrophe could strike whether it's in the shape of a mishap, wind storm or break-in. It is necessary that you understand that you have insurance coverage with a trustworthy company that's quick to settle your claim. Ensure the insurance provider has an excellent credibility for claim payout, and that they are recognized for being responsible.

6. How to Protect Your Car Throughout Storage

In case you will store your car for a month or more, it is essential that you stop unneeded repair work and damage from happening.

- Top off the gas tank to prevent/decrease condensation from having the ability to build up in the gas tank. Include a fuel stabilizer, then drive around the block to disperse it across the engine parts.

- To shield the car, wax and wash prior to storing.

- Put a 4-mil polyethylene drop cloth on the flooring to function as a vapor barrier.

- Disengage your parking brake to help with minimizing deterioration.

- Place your car on jack stands. This is going to remove the weight of the tires and wheels.

- Disconnect and get rid of the battery. You could put the battery on a trickle battery charger, or you could drain the battery periodically, with a little light bulb, and after that, utilize a low volt battery charger to charge it.

- Utilize a rag to plug the tailpipe to protect against damp air.

Your Car Interior

Your car's interior requires particular attention to remain looking as great as it did when it came off the production line.

- Park in the Shade-- A garage constantly provides the ideal location to park your vehicle, however, when a garage isn't an option, you could decrease damage from heat and UV sunshine by parking in the shade. In case there isn't any shade or in case you are getting a lot of bird droppings from parking beneath the tree, buy a vehicle shade to optimize your protection. This is additionally going to maintain your vehicle cooler.

- Clean the Interior-- Routinely rub down the interior whenever you clean your vehicle. Dirt particles, abrasive liquids, and spilled fluids like soda pop could be harsh and induce damage. You could clean up utilizing moderate detergent and water. You ought to additionally vacuum every time. You ought to rub the dust from the dash gauges and the lenses. Do not administer excessive pressure, or it is going to result in scratches.

- Utilize Flooring Mats-- Flooring mats could shield your car's carpeting, specifically throughout the winter season, when there is salt, slush, and even mud. The waffle style mats do not slip, and they are simple to clean off and vacuum.

7. Protect Your Windows And Door Seals

Initially wash with water and soap, then utilize a rubber protectant such as Armor All ® or a silicone-based product on the doors and windows to maintain them conditioned and to prevent them from drying. You must never ever utilize an item which is oil-based like WD-40 ®, which could harm your rubber.

In case your weather removing is making it possible for the water to drip into the interior, it's time to have it changed or fixed. The majority of little leakages could be fixed with a brush-on seam sealer. Fix torn part with a particular rubber caulking which could be bought at most car parts shops.

8. Stop Leather from Drying and Breaking

Leather interiors are abundant and long-lasting, in case they are kept effectively, however, when overlooked, they rapidly end up being split and unattractive. The leather ends up being stained with time. You ought to utilize a leather cleaner to eliminate dirt, and after that, follow that up with a leather protectant which is going to withstand discolorations, and maintain your leather soft and flexible. It is additionally going to make it simpler to clean up in the future.

9. Taking care of Upholstery

In case you have an upholstered interior, any car upholstery cleaner or house upholstery cleaner could be utilized. You will not require much as you do not wish to, in fact, soak the fabric. Administer, and then rub off with a tidy fabric. In case the fabric has a nap, utilize a brush to raise the texture back up.

Using a fabric protector like Scotchgard ™ is going to aid the upholstery to withstand dirt and minimize discolorations. It is additionally going to make it simpler to clean up the following time. Prior to using a fabric protector, you ought to clean up the fabric.

To decrease the staining from kids riding in kid seats, take a towel and put it beneath the car seat, or you could utilize a bit of heavy upholstery plastic.

Your Car's Exterior

- Shielding Automobile Paint From the Sun-- When your paint appears great, your car looks excellent. However, when subjected to the sun's ultraviolet rays, it could start to break the paint down and induce it to fade. A garage is your initial line of defense; however, the majority of us do not have a garage. The second ideal thing is to utilize a car cover, which could shield it from the elements.

10. Cleaning Your Vehicle

Cleaning your car makes it appear good, however, it has a far more crucial function, which is getting rid of the debris and dirt which could scrape your paint's surface. You ought to additionally clean your car throughout the winter season so the road salt, sand, and slush are removed before they can harm your paint finish. It's best if you could go to a car wash; however, it could be carried out at home with a warm water bucket provided that the temperature level is higher than zero. Utilize a mild soap developed for cleaning your automobile. At least a couple of times a year, you ought to utilize rim and tire cleaner.

11. Waxing Shields Your Vehicle

Wax is vital to your vehicle's paint. It makes the paint appear brand-new, and it additionally decreases oxidation, and it produces a barrier which shields your paint from sap, contamination, bird droppings, and so on. Here's what to do to obtain the ideal protection:

- While fluid waxes might be appealing due to the fact that you could get a good glossy vehicle with a lot less work, the point is that paste wax is more powerful, tougher, and lasts a lot more. Try to find a paste that's high in carnauba wax.

- Next, by utilizing a sponge, administer a really thin coat of wax to the paint. Ensure it's even, and do not apply it too thick (a typical error). If you apply it too thick, it's truly difficult to get rid of all of the residue.

A soft fabric works ideally to get rid of the dry wax. It will not scrape the paint.

- Due to the fact that the wax on the hood deteriorates faster from the engine heat, it's an excellent idea to use an additional couple of wax coats.

12. Place a Brand-new Skin on Your Vehicle

Paint is susceptible, however, there is a method to shield the locations which have a tendency to get the most stone chips utilizing a self-adhesive urethane film. These urethane films are ideal when used professionally; nevertheless, if you are handy at this kind of thing, you could give it a go personally. 3M ™ and Scotchgard ™ are both good choices. Once it's administered to the car, you could wax and clean as usual.

13. Touch up Chips

Even as we are ultra-careful, chips appear. Touch-up paint is an option, and for more recent cars, it's quite simple to compare colors. Utilize touch up paint to touch up chips before the rust is able to start to rust.

14. Quick Repair Work for Light Covers

In case you find yourself with a broken taillight cover or turn signal, you could change the whole thing. You could utilize tape for the fix, which is going to hold you over before you can appropriately fix it. You need to utilize the red or orange tape which is produced for this. Others are not going to adhere.

15. Changing Bulbs Effectively

As you are switching out burnt-out bulbs, clean the dirt away. In case the socket has actually ended up being rusty, utilize a little steel wool or wire brush to clean away rust. Then rub away the debris and set up the replacement bulb.

16. Fixing Little Chips in the Windscreen

Rock chips or fractures in the windscreen could hinder visibility, and when left ignored, they have a tendency to get much bigger when temperature levels change. It's a lot more affordable to stop into the windscreen repair shop and have a chip or fracture fixed, which brings back the initial glass integrity and maintains clear visibility.

17. When Hauling on the Roof

You may be lured to load up your roof. Inspect your owner's handbook for your car's specs. It's generally someplace in between 150 to 200 pounds or 68 to 90 kg. What does that mean? That's approximately eighteen 8' 2x4's or 3 3/4" plywood sheets. To shield the roof, you could put a blanket or a piece of cardboard down. You could additionally buy a luggage rack set.

18. Fasten Your Load

Constantly ensure your load is fastened to shield your vehicle's paint from being dented or scratched. It pays to purchase the appropriate cargo, bike or luggage racks. You could additionally utilize cargo straps and put a blanket initially to shield the car's surface.

19. Examine your Wheel Well Splashguards

Splashguards are created to maintain slush and water from sprinkling up into the engine compartment doing harm to electrical elements. Generally, these splashguards are rather lightweight and are frequently peeled without the driver knowing. You ought to examine these guards regularly, and in case they are loose, refasten or replace them.

Tires, Wheels, and Brakes

20. Look For Unequal Tire Wear

When tire inflation is preserved, and you still experience irregular wear, it might suggest that you require a wheel alignment. It could additionally suggest that you have actually been poorly utilizing your brakes, worn bushings, inner tire damage, shock issues, or a bent wheel.

21. Inspect Tire Tread

Various nations have various requirements concerning tread. In The United States, all tires sold need to have "wear bars" formed into the tires. This renders it simple to understand when tires need to be lawfully changed. The basic guideline is that when the tread is worn down to 1 1/16" or 1.5 mm, the tires have to be changed.

22. Maintain Caps on Valves

One little piece could induce a lot of sorrow. When the valve cap goes missing, it could result in a leakage. These caps stop wetness and dirt from entering. Inspect your valve caps and ensure they are not harmed or lacking. When you have tires changed, ask the store to make sure the tires have brand-new valves.

23. Have Tires Properly Inflated

Ensure your tires are correctly pumped up. When tires are under-inflated, it induces extreme tension and heat which could lead to tire failure. To get the most life out of your tires, buy a pressure gauge to ensure that you are able to examine your tires routinely. Once a month is suggested, however, throughout hot weather, it ought to be done more frequently. For a precise reading, check when the car has actually been driven less than a mile and when the tires are cold. Inflate based upon the producer's suggestions.

24. Do the Wet Thumb Test

As you are utilizing a service station air pump, prior to pumping the air in your tire, depress the inflator valve pin with your thumb. You are looking for wetness. If your thumb ends up being damp, enter into a service station, and allow the personnel understand the tank has to be drained. Locate another service station. Why is this so crucial? Well, due to the fact that if that wetness gets caught in the tire, it could result in variations in the tire pressure, and it could additionally rust rims.

25. Turn Your Tires

Routine tire turning helps to make sure that the tires wear out equally, and it is going to result in the optimum tire life. Your initial rotation is really essential. Your owner's handbook is going to offer you with a rotation duration and pattern. If you can't find this schedule, then turn your tires every 6000 to 7500 miles.

26. Tire Inflation and Temperature Level

The temperature level impacts tire pressure. When the temperature levels soar or drop, your tire pressure goes down. With underinflated tires, they are able to wear quicker and lead to bad driving

27. Utilizing Wheel Cleaner

Your wheels take a pounding due to being in contact with the roadway. Mix that with brake dust, and you have actually got some hard spots to get rid of. Routine car wash soap simply can't get rid of this gunk and grit. You want to utilize a cleaner which is particularly created for discolorations. There are various wheel cleaner formulas for various wheel finishes like aluminum and chrome. You could additionally include a protection layer by utilizing wax on painted wheels and wheel polish on metal wheels.

28. Lubricate the Lug Nuts

If you do not periodically lube your lug nuts they are going to seize to the studs due to rust. Repair work could be pricey, and if you have a blowout, you might find yourself in the requirement of a tow. Every time you turn your tires, it's an excellent idea to utilize an anti-seize lube, which you could purchase at your regional auto shop. Utilize a wire brush to clean up the studs, and then use the lube. It's created to prevent lug nuts from seizing while simultaneously stopping them from working their way off as you are driving. In case you do end up with a seized lug nut, attempt squirting WD-40 or Liquid Wrench on the impacted lug nut. Wait 10 to 30 minutes for it to permeate. After that, utilize your ratchet to get rid of the lug nut.

29. Stop the Hubcap Loss

Hubcaps end up being ruined, work themselves loose, and can then disengage themselves from your vehicle. They could be pricey to change. You could stop this from occurring by:

- Newer plastic hubcaps that are held in spot by a retaining wire ring which you snap into the wheel tables. Be cautious not to break or flex these tables.

- When it comes to the older metal hubcaps, pry the metal clips only somewhat outwards. This ought to deal with any problems.

- Utilize a rubber mallet and tap carefully as you go around the hubcap in a circle. Do not strike too much since you'll damage the clips.

30. Have a Routine Wheel Alignment

Wheel alignments are necessary. When your wheels are not aligned appropriately, your tires are going to wear out quicker, you'll have poorer handling, and it could induce wear to the pinion or rack or other steering elements. Refer to your owner's handbook for the advised schedule, or else, at least have your wheel alignment examined annually. In case you have a 4x4, or you do a great deal of off-road, have your wheel alignment inspected more frequently. If your car pulls to the left or right, have your wheel alignment done.

31. Top Off Your Brake Fluid

You ought to inspect your brake fluid monthly. Before opening the master cylinder cover, rub away any dust. If you have to include fluid, refer to the producer's suggestions. You must never ever swap liquids. For instance, never ever utilize power steering fluid instead of brake fluid. Never ever utilize brake fluid which had been opened, since as soon as it has actually been subjected to air, it could end up being polluted fast.

32. Taking care of Your Anti Lock Brakes

The anti-lock brake system in contemporary vehicles is sensitive to wetness, which could quickly ruin the pricey ABS pump and induce the interior of the brake lines to rot. Given that brake fluid have a tendency to draw in wetness every number of years, your brake lines ought to be bled. They are going to additionally be inspected when you have your yearly wheel alignment check. If you have a 4x4 or you devote a lot of time off-road, have them examined more frequently.

Vehicle Engine and Related Systems

33. Examine Your Oil

This is extremely crucial!

- Begin by draining your old oil.

- Then tidy the drain plug on the oil pan, and clean it off before re-installing your oil plan.

- To inspect your oil, operate your vehicle for at least 15 minutes to ensure that the oil heats up.

- Park the vehicle on level ground.

- Switch the engine off, wait for 15 minutes so that the oil is able to drain back to the oil pan.

- Get rid of the dipstick and rub it until it's clean.

- Reinsert it and press all of it the way in.

- Once again, yank the dipstick out and check the oil level.

- It ought to be someplace in between the hash marks. If in the add region, include oil based upon your producer's specs.

34. Change the Oil

Today's producers suggest a longer duration in between oil changes, but the truth is that more frequently abrasive dirt and metal particles are taken out from your engine, the longer it is going to purr like a kitty. It prolongs your engine's life. If you wish to optimize your engine, refer to the schedule for long periods in your owner's handbook. This is essential if you drive in stop-and-go traffic routinely. For several years it was suggested that your oil should be changed every 3000 miles. Those periods are expanding, however, there's no danger in adhering to the old numbers.

35. Which Oil to Utilize

There are a variety of oils in the marketplace. Let's take a look at them them.

- Detergent Oil-- Nearly all contemporary multi-weight oils are detergent oils, which get rid of soot from the interior engine parts, and after that, hold those oil particles. These particles are too small to end up being caught by the oil filter, so they remain drifting in the oil. This is why your oil remains darker. These particles do not harm your engine. Nevertheless, when the oil ends up being saturated, it can't keep on holding these tiny particles. Existing oil modification schedules take place before this takes place.

- Oil Viscosity-- The oil viscosity is defined by utilizing 2 numbers. The initial number is the viscosity when the oil is cold. You are then going to notice the letter W accompanied by another number. The W represents "winter." The majority of people believe it means weight. Then, there is another number, which informs you of the viscosity when the oil is at operating temperature level. The oil thickens as the number grows.

- Climate Considerations-- Your owner's handbook is going to note which oils are appropriate to utilize at various temperature levels. For instance, in case you reside in a warm climate, 10W30 is an appropriate alternative to 5W30. Previously, there was a summertime oil and winter season oil. That's the case no longer. Nevertheless, in case you reside in a warm climate, and you are utilizing 10W30, then make certain you change to 5W30 for the winter.

36. Changing the Oil Filter

As you change your oil, you are additionally going to alter your oil filter. It is best to stick to what the producer advises for the filter, however afterward additionally other filers offered by businesses like Pennzoil, Valvoline, Motorcraft, and a lot more. These filters are going to match the maker's filters. Remember that the quality of producer's filters is much higher than the market filters.

There are additionally trade brand name filters, that are located at much of the quick oil change locations. For those who utilize artificial oil, premium filters are typically utilized. They are pricier, however, the advantages have actually been confirmed.

37. Changing the Fuel Filter

Recently makers have actually been telling us that we do not have to meddle with our fuel filters so frequently. We still advise changing your fuel filter at least yearly. When a fuel filter becomes obstructed, it is going to induce your engine to perform badly, and it is going to lower your gas mileage. It's additionally an indication that a gas tank is starting to rust. You are going to see those particles in the filter.

38. Enhance Gas Mileage with a Clean Air Filter

Inspect your air filter every handful of months, and when it's unclean, change it. Air filters are simple to change. With a carbureted car, you simply get rid of the huge metal cover. With fuel-injected vehicles, you get rid of the rectangle-shaped box. Your handbook is going to demonstrate to you precisely where it is.

39. Have a Healthy Transmission

It is necessary to alter your transmission liquid after the initial 5,000 miles in a brand-new vehicle, and after that, each time your mileage is around 25,000 miles.

40. Never Ever Overfill the Crankcase

Do not overfill your crankcase with oil, since if you do, air bubbles are going to form in the oil, and after that, the oil pump is not going to have the ability to work appropriately. This could result in an engine getting too hot and stress being placed on a variety of engine parts. It could additionally trigger fouled sparkplugs.

41. Remember Your PCV Valve

The positive crankcase ventilation (PCV) valve is a component of the emissions system in older vehicles. The valve's task is to re-circulate partly burned gases from the engine crankcase to the combustion chamber. It's extremely vital, and it ought to be changed every 30,000 miles. It additionally assists in enhancing gas mileage by stopping the accumulation of sludge and rust.

42. In case You Tow, You Wish to Have an Oil Cooler

If you utilize your car to tow a trailer of some sort, you ought to have an oil cooler set up. You might additionally set up a transmission cooler. They are simple to set up, they don't cost much, and spare you big bucks when it comes to transmission and engine repairs.

43. New Spark Plugs Equate To Better Gas Mileage

Electronic ignitions, and vehicles with computer systems on board have actually gotten rid of the requirement for a routine tune-up. Nevertheless, it is still crucial to change your spark plugs routinely. The majority of makers advise changing your spark plugs every 30,000 to 40,000 miles. Excellent spark plugs aid your engine in carrying out much better, and you'll delight in better gas mileage.

44. Inspect the Hoses

Hoses end up being fragile and could break with time. When the vehicle is turned off and has actually cooled, pinch the hoses. If they are incredibly stiff, make a crunching noise, have bulges, are delicate or sticky, or appear collapsed in any part, it indicates the hose is fragile and ought to be changed. You must never ever drive with a compromised coolant hose because your engine might get too hot, and you might end up with an extremely pricey repair work bill.

45. Belt Tension

You ought to examine the belt tensions. You ought to additionally look for wear. You'll discover belts which run your Air Conditioning compressor, water pump, and power steering pump. To look for tension, push in the middle of the belt where the lengthiest exposed part is. In case you are able to depress the belt 1/2" to 1" or 13mm to 25mm, however no more than that, the tension is fine. Otherwise, you can either take your vehicle to a car shop for a change, or if you are proficient, you can do it on your own. Look for fractures and fraying, which indicate that you ought to change the belt(s).

46. Proactively Check the Timing Belt

Your handbook is going to tell you when you ought to change the timing belt at 50,000 miles; however, it does differ. When a timing belt stops working, it could lead to countless dollars of damage to the engine, so it's ideal to be proactive.

47. The Engine Cleaning

It's a great idea to perform an engine clean every handful of years. By getting rid of all the gunk and dirt, it ends up being a lot easier to see any leakages. When cleaning your car, keep in mind not to soak crucial engine parts like electrical parts or distributor caps. You could use plastic bags to cover them. Liquid dish soap functions effectively to cut grease. There are additionally lots of outstanding grease-cutting detergents on the marketplace.

Car Battery, Air Conditioning, and Other Crucial Parts

48. Switch Your Air Conditioning on in Winter season

If you assume I have actually lost my mind, I have not. You ought to turn your Air Conditioning on at least a number of times in the winter season to stop your Air Conditioning compressor from seizing.

49. Preserving Your Vehicle Battery

It is necessary for your vehicle battery to be in good shape, and for this to occur, you ought to do a routine upkeep. Maintaining your vehicle battery isn't that challenging.

- It starts with maintaining your battery tidy. Rub with a moist rag utilizing moderate dish detergent.

- Clean the terminals or battery posts -- initially get rid of the negative cable, and then the positive one. Red = positive, Black = negative. Soak a brass wire battery brush into water and baking soda blend. Only a couple of tablespoons of baking soda included in a bit of water, and you are going to have the appropriate combination.

- Look for fractures on the battery itself. Additionally, look for bulging. These are indications that the battery has to be changed.

- Re-install your battery cables beginning with the positive.

50. Preserving Your Battery

In case a battery has a vent cap, you'll wish to get rid of it and examine the electrolyte level. It has to cover the battery's leading plates by at least a 1/2" or 13mm. You must not utilize faucet water due to the fact that it could have minerals which might harm your battery. Rather, utilize distilled water.

51. Sealing a Leaky Radiator

In case you have a radiator which is dripping, there are a several radiator sealants which can be found in a liquid or powder form. These items distribute through the radiator, and when they reach the hole, the item gets in contact with air and creates a seal.

52. Water down the Coolant

Your cooling system needs to consist of water and coolant-antifreeze. You do not utilize undiluted coolant. Usually, the mix is a 50/50 ratio. You must additionally never ever utilize straight water in your radiator. Inspect your coolant-antifreeze at least a number of times per month and ensure you have ample coverage throughout cold weather to guarantee that your radiator does not freeze.

53. You Need To Flush Coolant

Coolant-antifreeze loses its potency and ends up being polluted. You have to flush your system every 2 years for certain coolants and every 5 years for others. Check out your coolant label for comprehensive instructions. In case you do not do a flush frequently, you run the risk of harming your radiator, and blocking the heating unit core. The water pump and thermostat can also stop working.

54. Never Ever Blend Your Coolants

You must never ever blend coolants of various colors. In case your coolant is pink, then do not include green coolant, since if you do, you are going to end up with a dense goop solution which can not do its work.

55. Inspect Power Steering Liquid

Each month you ought to examine your power steering fluid once the vehicle has actually heated up. If the level is low, you ought to have the hoses and pump checked for any kind of leakage. If the power steering fluid is low, you could harm the power steering pump.

Chapter 6: How to Have a Healthy Fuel System

The fuel system is vital to your vehicle working efficiently. The fuel system provides the engine with the diesel/gas it needs to operate, and if any part of the fuel system isn't operating appropriately, it can cause significant issues.

The Fuel Sending Unit

This is where fuel is helpful. The fuel gets to the tank by means of the filler tube. There is a sending system which sends out information back to your gauge concerning the quantity of fuel you have. In case this sending unit ceases working, you are not going to get a precise reading of just how much fuel you have. In case the fuel gauge quits working, the issue is going to be either with the fuel sending system or with the gauge itself.

The Fuel Pump

In the more recent cars, the fuel pump is generally within the fuel tank. On older cars, it is connected to the frame rail or the engine. In case the fuel pump starts to malfunction, your car can tumble and run extremely roughly. If the fuel pump falls short, your car is not going to work. Many contemporary fuel pumps could be heard as you turn the ignition key. In case you do not hear the pump working and your vehicle doesn't get going, it might be your fuel pump.

Fuel Filter

A tidy fuel filter is necessary for the functionality of your engine and its life span. Fuel injectors have extremely small openings which could rapidly end up being obstructed, so the fuel filter prevents these particles from making it through. If your car has high mileage, alter the fuel filter each year. For brand-new cars, follow the producer's instructions. Indications of a blocked fuel filter consist of the engine not starting or faltering at high speeds. This is the most typical issue with the fuel system.

Fuel Injectors

Since 1986 the majority of domestic vehicles have actually been fuel injected. The fuel injector is a small electrical valve, which is shut and opened by an electrical signal. Unclean injector forms in time as deposits slip by the fuel filter. This could induce fuel injectors to stick open, sending out excessive fuel to the engine, or they can end up being plugged, sending out insufficient fuel to the engine.

Using a routine fuel system cleaner assists in maintaining the injectors clean and could be acquired at department stores, car shops, and many filling stations. Place it in your empty tank and fill it after that. This is going to clean your injectors. Redo this every 3 months.

Where You Purchase Gas is Important

You might be shocked to discover that it is not important where you purchase your gas. You ought to constantly buy from a well recognized nationwide brand name. Gas stations without any association purchase what's left on a truck when the day ends, and the combination could make some cars run horribly. Additionally, any water in the gas is going to induce your engine to run badly, and it is going to promote rust progression in your fuel system.

When it pertains to octane, increasing the octane is throwing the cash away unless the vehicle maker particularly advises it. You are not going to get better gas mileage or much better functionality. For the majority of us, the most affordable octane at the pump is all that the car needs.

Last Minute Fuel Tips

- When you park in the sun, you are going to experience fuel loss because of evaporation, so park in the shade.

- Make certain you secure your gas cap.

- When your cap is loosened, or absent, gas is going to evaporate, so make certain your cap is tight.

- Don't bother rounding off your gas tank. When the automated nozzle clicks off, quit pumping, or else it is going to splash around and leak out.

- Effectively inflated tires point to much greater gas mileage. Underinflated tires point to inferior gas mileage.

- Make sure your engine is tuned up. An effectively tuned car can enhance your gas mileage by approximately 5%. A misfiring spark plug could lower your fuel efficiency by as much as 30%.

Chapter 7: Body Care Tips

Maintaining your car looking terrific does not need to be difficult. Even an old car could appear like brand-new one with routine care. We have actually all seen those collector vehicles which have never ever been repainted. Your car's paint could appear that excellent years from now as well.

Cleaning Your Vehicle

Wash your car at least one time a month. Bugs, limestone, bird droppings-- they could all leave irreversible spots on your paint if not cleaned off. The wetness rapidly dries on a tidy car; however, when the car is unclean, the wetness collects in the unclean places, which can cause deterioration. It's ideal to utilize a washing item developed for the paint on your car.

At least from time to time, you ought to additionally utilize a pressure washer. The ones at the coin car washes function effectively. The pressure washer has the ability to deal with dirt in tough places. Do not place the pressure water very close to the paint as it could induce peeling.

Waxing Your Automobile

Wax your automobile routinely. The wax makes your automobile lovely and glossy, and it shields the paint from environmental aspects, fading and discoloration. It takes just around an hour to wax a whole vehicle. An excellent wax is going to last around 3 months. By waxing your vehicle only 4 times per year, you could make sure your paint looks brand-new.

There are a lot of wax items in the marketplace. So many that it could be mind-boggling attempting to choose one. Staying with a carnauba car wax is a great option. It is simple to use and holds up effectively.

How to Fix a Stone Chip

If you do not fix a stone chip on your paint fast, it is going to start to rust. It's not as hard as it might appear.

- Head to your dealer to match a spray paint to your car's paint color.

- Wash the automobile and allow it to dry.

- Get your spray paint and shake properly.

- You'll additionally require a sharp wooden stick.

- Spray a tiny amount into the cap.

- Soak the stick in the cap.

- Put the stick end into the chip and dab.

Chapter 8: Tips for a Good Automatic Transmission

Become Well Acquainted With Your Automatic Transmission and Have it Serviced

Your auto transmission transports the engine power to the drive wheels utilizing a series of gear sets, bands and clutches. The transmission brain is the valve body, which reacts to either electrical or hydraulic signals which tell the transmission when to move. The pump is the core of the transmission supplying the hydraulic pressure required for lubrication and administering the required quantity of lubrication to friction devices. The transmission is the most complicated part of your car's whole drive shaft. There are more than 1,000 moving parts, and every one needs to operate perfectly for the following piece to run properly.

With a lot of moving parts, it's not difficult to comprehend why upkeep is so essential. Invest om routine filter and fluid changes and evaluations, and you'll spare countless dollars in repairs. There is absolutely nothing low-cost about fixing a transmission.

10 Ways to Extend Your Transmissions Life

1. Frequently inspect transmission fluids. See the owner's handbook for servicing particulars.

2. Examine the transmission liquid when it has actually been running hot. Stop and go traffic, uneven terrain, hauling a trailer, and hot weather could all result in extreme transmission heat which could result in the fluid loss, fluid damage, or both. You ought to frequently inspect the fluid when the transmission has actually run hot. By routinely, I am talking about the very next filling station.

3. Set up an external cooler. In case you find yourself continually stuck in traffic, haul a trailer, or frequently haul heavy loads, that could cause extreme heat. An external transmission cooler carries the transmission temperature level down

into the regular operating range, prolonging your transmissions life.

4. Change transmission liquid frequently when the car is utilized in high-stress conditions. Your transmission liquid is developed to cool the transmission and to lube the transmission parts while offering the hydraulic pressure so all the elements can interact. When the transmission fluid is no more able to perform these activities effectively, the life of the transmission is substantially reduced. In case your car runs under high-stress conditions, it's a great idea to alter the transmission liquids two times a year.

5. Have the transmission linkage inspected and calibrated frequently. This is crucial for cars under a heavy workload.

6. Immediately have malfunctions inspected. Transmission repair work expenses increase in relation to how long the car is driven after the initial indications of difficulty. The longer you disregard a transmission which is breaking down, the more you can anticipate the repairs to cost.

7. Ensure your engine is correctly tuned. In case your engine is not operating correctly, the signs can, in some cases, resemble transmission problems.

8. Have drive train parts frequently examined. There are some drive train parts that are connected directly to the transmission operating. Universal joints, drive axles, continuous speed joints, driveshafts, flywheels, flexplates, computer systems, cooling systems, transmission mounts, engine mounts, and sensing units all contribute to your transmission operating appropriately.

9. Inspect cooling system two times a year. Have your cooling system inspected for correct coolant strength, leakages and levels. Antifreeze degrades gradually, so it has to be changed to keep its performance.

10. Each year have a total physical done on your car. Every year, your car ought to be examined from top to bottom, involving steering, brakes, lights, and other safety parts.

20 Signs of Potential Transmission Issues

There are all sorts of things which could occur to transmission, and a lot of these repairs could be really expensive. There are a number of signs which suggest that there might be transmission issues later on. Let's take a look at the top 20 signs.

1. When the car is cold, and you place it into driver, there is a hold-up. The car shifts late throughout an initial couple of minutes of operation.

2. The shifter does not enter into drive or reverse. You put the shifter into a driver (D) or reverse (R), yet absolutely nothing occurs.

3. Fresh discolorations beneath your car.

4. You can not get the shifter to enter any position. Even when the engine is racing, it does not budge.

5. Shifting takes place at the incorrect speed levels leading to premature or late shifting.

6. Slippage. The engine rpm is high; however, the car goes extremely sluggishly, and it doesn't speed up.

7. Not able to place into passing gear, or it enters into overdrive, however, there is no rise in power when you apply the gas.

8. Rough shifting leads to a rough sensation or clunking when the transmission is placed into gear.

9. Unpredictable shifting. Velocity, when shifting takes place, is never ever the same.

10. There is a burning odor or putrid odor.

11. Engine braking does not work in several positions.

12. The car tries to move when in the park.

13. Service engine light or check light keeps coming on.

14. Car stalls during taking off.

15. The shifter sign doesn't point to the appropriate gear any longer.

16. The shifter has actually ended up being tough to move into a position or out of it.

17. You hear unusual sounds. Groans, grunts, hisses, and so on.

18. The shifter sign is somewhat off neutral (N) and/or park (P) when you go to turn on the vehicle.

19. When checked, there is a significant quantity of filings and debris in the transmission pan.

20. Shifting suddenly.

Things You Must Not do if You Wish to Extend Your Transmissions Life

1. Never ever leave your car in the park without placing your parking brake on. If your car was even simply tapped by another car, it might lead to the parking pawl, a part within your transmission, breaking, and your car rolling because of that. When ignored, this might induce considerable harm.

2. Never ever brake by downshifting. It's a usual practice to downshift at traffic lights instead of utilizing brakes. A forced downshift at a greater RPM result in unnecessary deterioration on the transmission bands and clutches.

3. Never ever change from drive into reverse when the engine is at a fast idle. This sudden transmission engagement could lead to malfunction of the

clutches, bands, gear sets, driveline elements, in addition to transmission and engine mounts.

4. Do not drag race. If your car was created for racing, that's great. However, stock transmissions and drivelines aren't developed for that kind of abuse or torque, and you might harm your transmission and a variety of driveline parts.

5. Never ever rock your automobile in the sand or snow. Get towed or dig yourself out; however, do not do that rocking from reverse to drive that you see many individuals doing. The extra heat which this induces could lead to burning your transmission out in a brief time period. A tow is far less expensive!

6. Do not drive up until your engine has actually heated up. For your transmission to be appropriately lubed, the fluid has to be at running temperature level. It might require you a couple of minutes longer to start; however, it is going to spare you a lot of cash.

7. Never ever tow your car with the drive wheels on the ground. Front-wheel drive cars need to have the front wheels in the air. Rear-wheel-drive cars need to be hauled with the back wheels off the ground. All-wheel or four-wheel drive cars have to be hauled flat. Refer to your owner's handbook for correct towing instructions to stay away from major harm.

8. Never ever stop all of a sudden. Abrupt stops (and quick starts) can lead to harm to your drive train and its elements consisting of engine mounts and transmission.

9. Do not attempt to repair your own transmission. Nonprescription quick fixes such as additives which are developed to stop leakages or make your transmission shift much better consist of a great deal of various chemicals which could induce seals that are currently used to become swollen, or they could impact the function of rubber parts which result in more severe damage. It does not pay to play around since you can induce more damage, and the end outcome is going to be a larger repair expense than what you would have paid if you had simply gone to the transmission store.

10. Get routine maintenance. Ensure your transmission obtains the routine servicing it requires to remain in great shape.

10 Sounds that Indicate You Might Have Transmission Issues

Your car has typical sounds which you end up being used to. When those sounds alter, you'll most likely observe it quite rapidly. If you experience a brand-new sound which you have actually not formerly heard, it might be the beginning of an issue. Here are the main 10 sounds you want to watch out for:

1. Clicking

2. Buzzing

3. Squealing

4. Groaning

5. Screeching

6. Humming in any gear

7. Grating in gear.

8. Clanking when put into reverse (R) or drive (D)

9. Chattering when put into reverse (R) or drive (D)

10. Rumbling in gear.

Chapter 9: How to Pick a Mechanic and a Car Repair Shop.

It is difficult to undrestand where to take your car if you believe you require repair work or upkeep. Let's take a look at what you ought to look for Experience.

Search for an auto store that has experience. Look duration of service and areas of expertise. For instance, if you require an engine repair work, you would opt for a mechanics store which has a track record for excellent work. If you require a transmission repair work, then you would like to know they are proficient in transmission repair work.

Dependability and Capability

Search for a service center with mechanics and specialists who are up to date with their training and attending workshops and remaining current. You additionally wish to take your vehicle to a store which has a track record for being trustworthy-- getting the work done on time.

BBB

It's a great idea to give the Better Business Bureau a call and learn whether the car center has actually had any grievances, and if so, which mechanic and what kind of grievances.

Check On the Internet

The Internet provides some great services regarding grading car mechanic shops. There are message boards, online forums, websites which rate car repair shops, and so on. There are numerous exceptional resources on the web. Make certain to make the most of them.

Request Recommendations

In the event where you might find yourself dealing with a big repair bill, do not hesitate to request references from the car service center. In case the garage chooses not to offer you references, you ought to search somewhere else.

Look for Accreditation

Ensure the mechanics are licensed in relevant areas. Seek to see how many accreditations the mechanic has. The more accreditations, the more probable it is that the mechanic is truly into what he works on and shows a genuine interest.

Ask Lots Of Questions

When you find yourself with a vehicle issue, do not hesitate to ask the service writer and/or mechanic questions. You most probably have worries, and you ought to have the ability to receive answers to ensure that you could confidently continue with getting the repair work done.

There you have it. Lots of excellent suggestions to assist you to keep your car looking and running fantastic. These pointers are going to leave you with money and time on your hands. Looking after your car indicates you can anticipate years of problem-free driving. What more could you ask for? An automobile that's dependable, trustworthy, and costs little to repair is everybody's dream. These ideas are going to aid you to get that vehicle.

I hope that you enjoyed reading through this book and that you have found it useful. If you want to share your thoughts on this book, you can do so by leaving a review on the Amazon page. Have a great rest of the day.

Printed in Great Britain
by Amazon

18374997R00048